as SU[TCH]

C000285957

The political manifesto of

THE OFFICIAL MONSTER RAVING LOONY PARTY

WARNING: VOTING CAN SERIOUSLY DAMAGE YOUR SANITY

Published by McNaughty Books, an imprint of John Napir Ltd P.O.Box 3353. London N1 1SR with assistance, as often, from Alwyn and Brad.

To Giselle, my partner, Tristan Lord Sutch, my son, Norma and Alan Hope, Deputy Lord Mayor of Ashburton and Proprietor of the Golden Lion Hotel Ashburton, our Official Headquarters, Alice's, Paul Barrett, Wild Willi Beckett, Valerie Bird, Danny Blandford, Mark Boyle, Alan Clayton, Mike and Babbs Delaney, Riaz Dooley - King of the Bucket Shops, Marie Duncan, Peter Frier, Bob Gilbert, Roly Gillard, Steve Golly, Melvin Hartshorne, the Custard Beast, Pat and Ken Hellier, Stan Herley, Ken What's Next, Tony King Mega Agent, Newt Kingston, Knutz, Joe Meek, T.C. Owen, Bananaman, International Press Cutting Bureau, John Repsch, Rockin' Dave Robbo, John and Jane Rowe, Charlie Salt, Sekonda Watches for the front and back cover, Graham Sharpe, Smiths of Gainsborough, Leyton Somers, Stan and Melanie Staniforth, Peter Stockton, The Strangerover, Stringfellows, John Tempest, The Press Association for all the black and white photographs, Baron Von Thunderclap, Lord of Tiverton, Vivienne Westwood, James Whale, Bob Winter, the late Henry Henderson, all past and present Savages, my Ma, Annie Sutch, who started it all off, and all those who have given thoughts and ideas and supported the Loony cause. Thanks and may your deposits be returned.

ISBN 1-898505-071

Printed and bound in the U.K.

CONTENTS

ARE YOU A LOONY?

Between now and May 1997, there will be a General Election. What a bore! Same old faces, same old policies, same old promises, same old lies. Isn't it time we told these tedious politicians what we think of them? Here's how it can be done:

VOTE

You may never have voted before (and why should you - they're all the same) But what if there was a Party dedicated to fun? There is. The Official Monster Raving Loony Party puts the fun back into politics, with fancy dress, rock 'n' roll gigs, publicity stunts, and a guaranteed Victory Party before the voting's even started! A vote for the

LOONY

Party is a way of saying to the other major parties: You're Boring! They won't like this. More reason to do it.

The Prime Minister Designate
© Wendy Jamieson

HOW TO VOTE

Voting is easy. Here's how to do it.

No. 1   Make sure you're on the Electoral Register. (You have to register by 10 October.)

No. 2   Wait for the dull grey John Major to consult his gnomes, the removal men and Norma, and name 'The Day'. If you miss his announcement - don't worry. The press, the radio and the TV will go on and on about 'The Day'. You won't be able to miss it, even though you'll want to.

No. 3   During the campaign, remember that all the other parties will be trying to buy your vote - with your own money.
The Loonies are different. We don't want to buy your vote - we only want to borrow it for 'The Day'. You can have it back afterwards.

No. 4   On the day before 'The Day' go to the Official Monster Raving Loony Victory Party and enjoy yourself hugely.

No. 5   On 'The Day' go to your local Polling Station and lend us your vote.

No. 6 There will be only one choice:

Conservative Party	greyish blue	No choice
'New' Labour **(née The Labour Party)**	greyish pink	No choice
Liberal Democrats	greyish bluey pink	No choice
Official Monster **Raving Loony Party**	FUN	**The** choice

No. 7 If you have any doubts, read this Manifesto again. (Don't bother with the others, they're far too dull.) If you agree with our policies, put a big **X** against the name of your Loony candidate. If you're not so sure, just put a little **x** instead.

No. 8 Go home, proud in the certain knowledge that you've done your democratic duty. Relax - you deserve to.

No. 9 Open another can or bottle, turn on the TV and roar with laughter at the shocked faces of the smug little politicians as they discover that Screaming Lord Sutch is on his way to . . .

7

YOU WANT POLITICS?
YOU GOT IT

You may have noticed that politicians are getting more coverage than ever in the media - but at the same time there's less politics than ever. That's because the unofficial parties don't believe in anything anymore. And even if they did, the leaders are too scared to put any real policies forward in case the opinion polls don't like them. So instead they just tinker with the edges of the economy, slag off their opponents and hope that no-one notices their impotence.

Meanwhile the Official Monster Raving Loony Party continues to break new ground, not only thinking the unthinkable, but also writing the unwritable and saying the unsayable.

Remember: what we propose today, the others will be copying tomorrow.

LAW AND ORDER

* All police officers will be issued with mountain bikes, except those in the Flying Squad who will be issued with space hoppers instead.
* We will solve the problem of over-crowding in prisons by releasing all the innocent prisoners.
* It is unfair that judges and barristers should have to wear fancy dress in court so that we all laugh at them. In the interests of equality we insist that everyone appearing in court should wear wigs and silly clothes.

WHY YOUR COUNTRY NEEDS LORD SUTCH

● **The Official Monster Raving Loony Party is the ONLY official party in Britain.**

> ● All the others are unofficial. That's why no-one takes them seriously.

● **Britain needs a Prime Minister with experience and authority.**

> ● Screaming Lord Sutch is the longest serving party leader in the country. He has led his party for thirty-three years.

> ● During that time the Tories have had five leaders, Labour have had six and the Liberals/Liberal Democrats/SDP/Alliance have had seven. Eighteen party leaders between them - how can they decide what's best for Britain when they can't even decide what's best for themselves?

● **Britain needs a Prime Minister for the whole country.**

> ● There are 659 constituencies. Only three of them are represented by the leaders of the three unofficial parties.

> ● Lord Sutch, on the other hand, has contested elections in a total of 39 constituencies. And he has won them all.

> ● He represents the entire nation: from Yeovil to Perth, from Brecon to Rotherham, from London to Liverpool - time and time again Lord Sutch has been the people's official choice as Prime Minister.

NATIONAL HEALTH SERVICE

* All British hospitals will be twinned with hospitals in other countries, so that you can decide where you want to convalesce.
* Wigs will be made available on the NHS and will then be made compulsory for all people who are losing their hair. Especially Tony Blair.
* Complimentary medicine should be available on the National Health Service. (We're not so sure about complementary medicine.)
* Placebos should be free at the point of use.

YOUTH

Actually we don't have any policies on youth. We think they're probably better off without politicians interfering with them.

JEFFREY ARCHER

We have conducted extensive research into the state of Britain today - its declining economic position, its failure to reach the final of Euro 96 or to win gold medals at the Olympics, and the Royal Family's inability to stay married. At the root of all these problems, we have discovered, is the sinister figure of Jeffrey Archer, whose books have sapped the country of its moral strength. He will therefore have to be abolished.

It's Never too Soony to Vote for a Loony

FOREIGN AFFAIRS

We believe that we are citizens of the world. Loonyism is not limited by national barriers; it's a state of mind.

*   We believe in freedom of movement around the world. People should be entitled to live wherever they want. Even if it's in Peckham, Walsall or Milton Keynes New Town.
*   Unlike the unofficial parties, we would welcome to this country victims of torture who are fleeing persecution (and they won't even need to bring certificates of authentication from their torturers).
*   We will also provide sanctuary for animals fleeing from persecution, particularly for: Spanish donkeys, French horses, Dutch veal calves, Australian watchetty grubs and mad anythings from anywhere.
*   We will ban imports of Liebfraumilch.
*   We know that the so-called United so-called States of so-called America are regretting their foolish decision to go it alone in 1776. In a spirit of forgiveness we will allow them to rejoin Great Britain and will give them full colonial status.

THE WINE LAKE

*   Every Sunday we propose to pump the Euro Wine lake through the Channel Tunnel to a pond or reservoir near you. Why we should pay for the E.C. Wine lake without benefiting is quite beyond ussh.

THIRTY YEARS OF UNBROKEN SUCCESS!

In every general election since the Loonies started standing, we have been
the largest party.

Unfortunately since many of our supporters go to Official Monster Raving
Loony Party Victory parties the night before, they wake up late with
enormous hangovers and forget where the polling booths are until it's all over.
Even those who don't go to the official celebrations organize their own
private parties to celebrate the overthrow of the grey forces of government.
So they're too hungover to vote as well.

Assuming that all those on the electoral register who didn't vote actually
meant to vote Loony but didn't quite make it to the booths in time, the results
of the last thirty years look like this:

	Tory	Labour	Liberal	Other	Loony
1966	32%	36%	6%	1%	24%
1970	33%	31%	5%	2%	28%
1974 (Feb)	30%	29%	15%	5%	21%
1974 (Oct)	26%	28%	13%	5%	27%
1979	33%	28%	10%	4%	24%
1983	31%	20%	18%	4%	27%
1987	32%	23%	17%	3%	25%
1992	33%	27%	14%	5%	22%

On these figures Britain is clearly a three-party state, and the Official Loonies
have nothing to fear from our unofficial rivals - we beat the Tories in 1974, we
spanked the Labour Party in 1983 and 1987, and we always thrash the
Liberals pantsdown.

THE SOCIAL CHAPTER

The social policies of the European Union don't go far enough. We promise:

* A twenty hour working week (in the new decimal time).
* A minimum wage fixed at 100% of MPs' salaries.
* Maternity and paternity leave for pets.

THE ECONOMY

* The Ecu will be replaced by the Yahoo, featuring a picture of the Official Prime Minister, Screaming Lord Sutch.

We have in fact formed the Official Opposition for fourteen of the last twenty-two years.

But these are statistics. And we all know that statistics lie. So what's the truth?

The shocking truth is that many of our natural supporters aren't even allowed to vote: prisoners, members of the House of Lords, people under 18 and those deemed by common law to be 'idiots' or 'lunatics' - all are excluded from politics in Britain.

Even more people have been disenfranchised by the inefficient bureaucracy of local councils. It is considered normal for electoral registers to have a margin of error of up to 4%. Even worse, in 1982 a government organization calculated that there was actually a 9% level of inaccuracy in the electoral register.

9%!!! That's over three million people who weren't on the rolls.
When these people are included in the Loony total (who else represents them?), it is clear that we've won every general election we've contested. And that's official.

IT'S A LOONY LANDSLIDE

SUPERSTITIONS

Superstition is the wisdom of the ages. We would be foolish to ignore the lessons it has to teach. We therefore propose a new Superstitions Act to enshrine this wisdom in British Law:

* It will be illegal to walk under ladders.
* Matches will be made with a capacity for lighting only two cigarettes.
* Umbrellas will not be opened indoors.
* All new houses will be built with an accessible piece of wood in each room for touching.
* Nobody will be allowed to refer to 'Macbeth' except as 'The Scottish Play'.
* Nobody should pick up a pair of scissors that they've dropped.
* Mirrors will be made of unbreakable glass.

A related Folklore Act will ensure that:

* Everybody looks before they leap.
* People should look after their pennies, while paying no attention to their pounds.
* Nobody watches a pot in case it doesn't boil.
* Many a mickle always makes a muckle.
* There are never too many cooks.
* Nobody is better than they ought to be.

THE OFFICIAL MONSTER RAVING LOONY PARTY

LOONOMETER

7.5 UNITS
of alcohol
200 SEATS

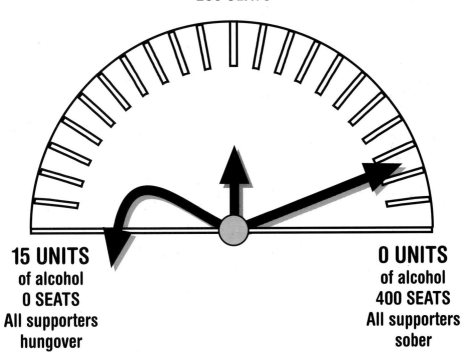

15 UNITS
of alcohol
0 SEATS
All supporters
hungover

0 UNITS
of alcohol
400 SEATS
All supporters
sober

THE GREAT AND THE GOOD

It has become traditional for political parties to claim the support of famous personalities: 'New' Labour has Melvyn Bragg, the Liberal Democrats have John Cleese and the Tories have the late Kenny Everett.

The lovely Joanna Lumley:
Loony supporter

Quite why this should make a blind bit of difference to normal punters is far from clear, but it seems that it's necessary in the modern world, so we're not going to be left out.

Here's some pictures of famous people.

The lovely Patrick Moore:
Loony supporter

The lovely Bob Geldof KBE:
'I'd vote for Sutch every time'

David Frost: Gold Card life-member
of the Official Monster Raving Loony Party

CULTURE AND HERITAGE

* We think culture's quite a good thing.
* But isn't French pop music crap?
* And German television.
* And Italian films.
* And Spanish literature.
* We will establish a fund to support the British film industry, to be called the Sam Kydd Memorial Fund.
* We shall redirect Lottery money from Covent Garden to New Covent Garden - fruit and vegetables are more important than ballet and opera.
* We shall launch a National Rock & Roll College where people can learn how to be roadies and the next Johnny Rotten.
* We shall abolish Damien Hirst.

AGONY AUNTS

* Anyone who writes a problem column in a national newspaper will be given a seat in the House of Lords, since they're so good at sorting out other people's problems and falling asleep.

WE WUZ ROBBED

Even though we have consistently been the most popular party in the country, we have never been invited by The Queen to form a government. But that doesn't mean we haven't had an influence on politics in Britain. Far from it. It just means that everybody else nicks our policies and claims them as their own:

● Votes at 18   Advocated by Lord Sutch
                          Stolen by Harold Wilson

● Votes at 16   Advocated by Lord Sutch
                          Stolen by the Liberal Democrats

● Commercial radio   Advocated by Lord Sutch
                          Stolen by Ted Heath

● Abolition of the 11+   Advocated by Lord Sutch
                          Stolen by the Labour Party

● All-day opening for pubs Advocated by Lord Sutch
                          Stolen by Margaret Snatcher

Today our policies continue to set the agenda:

● Passports for pets
   - Under consideration by the European Commission

● Special ramps at the back of busses for the elderly and disabled
   - Tried out by Transport Secretary Stephen Norris in 1995

CONSTITUTIONAL REFORM

* Shamefully Lord Sutch has never been allowed to take his place in the House of Lords. Nor were Duke Ellington, Count Basie or Lord Rockingham. We will end this discrimination against musicians.

* We will make elections more democratic. In the 1983 general election the Official Monster Raving Loony Party fielded eleven candidates - all of them were the official winners, including Lord Sutch, who beat Margaret Thatcher in Finchley. In a fit of bad temper Thatcher then decided that it should cost people £500 to stand for parliament.
  This is an appaling tax on democracy - we will reduce the deposit to one Yahoo.

* Opinion polls will be banned during elections because they're too boring. Instead daily odds - compiled by Lord Sutch's favourite bookmaker Mr William Hill - will be quoted on all TV news broadcasts.

* We will introduce votes at 16.

* And votes for pets.

* And at every election people will get a chance to vote for the next general election as well, so that if they die in between they can leave their vote in their will.

*'No,' says Harold. 'There will be no commercial radio,
and you should get a haircut!'*

But he was wrong!

DECIMAL TIME

Current time-keeping is too confusing - especially when you're hungover, late for work and trying to figure out a 24-hour timetable.

* We will simplify the system. There will be 100 seconds to a minute, 100 minutes to an hour, 10 hours per day, 10 days per week, 5 weeks per month and 10 months in the year.
* We will abolish January and February. The weather will therefore be better with virtually no winter. And the NHS will save money because there will be fewer people getting colds and flu.

STATE OF EMERGENCY

We checked out the legal position on this one and it's constitutionally okay for the Queen to declare a State of Emergency, suspend parliament, withdraw from Europe and from NATO and to rule directly from Buckingham Palace. We shall, however, advise the Queen to invoke these powers only if:

* Cliff Richard releases a Christmas single,
* Barbara Cartland dies, or
* we don't win the general election.

AGRICULTURE

* We shall fund research into why crop-circles never appear in turnip fields.

THE LOONY LEGACY

Throughout history there have been Loony politicians hard at work in Britain and all over the world laying the foundations of a Loony society. We shall build on this glorious legacy:

● In 1649 Christmas was abolished by Act of Parliament.
  - We shall abolish Christmas singles by Cliff Richard.

● Until 1819 you could be hanged for cutting down a tree.
  - We shall revive this noble law for cable TV companies who destroy urban trees.

● Football was banned in the 16th century because it was too violent.
  - We shall ban synchronized swimming because it's not violent enough.

And we'll enforce all the Loony laws that are still in existence in Britain, but which have fallen into disuse:

● Every citizen will once again be obliged to practise archery on Sundays.

● All taxi-drivers will have to carry a bale of hay in their cabs for their horses.

● Nobody will be allowed to send red envelopes through the post.

● Fortune-telling is still illegal in Britain so - regrettably - we shall have to abolish Mystic Meg.

William Hill's commitment to democracy found its greatest expression in 1995. When Lord Sutch was threatened with bankruptcy, Mr Hill offered to pay all his election expenses so he could continue his political career.

MINISTRY FOR PETS

Now that pets have votes they will need representation.

* We will create a Minister for Pets, whose first Bill will be a Dangerous Politicians Act - certain politicians will not be allowed out unless on a lead and muzzled. And some Tory MPs will obviously have to be neutered.

DEFENCE

* Contrary to popular opinion, it is not the policy of the Official Monster Raving Loony Party to spend vast quantities of British money on nuclear weapons so that we can kill everybody 200 times. That's the policy of the unofficial loonies in the Tory Party, 'New' Labour and Liberal Democrats. We think blowing up the world once is enough.

INTERNATIONAL LOONYISM

As John Donne said 'No Loony is an island'. Not even in Britain, which is an island. Many of our comrades in the Loonyist International have been doing sterling work over the years, persuading their politicians to introduce loony legislation. Amongst their achievements are:

● A law in Kentucky says everyone has to have a bath at least once a year.

● In Iraq it's illegal to eat snakes on Sundays.

● In New York City it is illegal for women to smoke in public.

● In Paraguay it's legal to have a duel, but only if both contestants are registered as blood donors.

● In Indiana it's forbidden to travel by bus within four hours of eating garlic.

● In Sienna it is illegal to be a prostitute - but only if your name's Mary.

● It's against the law in Arizona to hunt camels.

● In Russia it's illegal to drive a dirty car.

An Official Working Party is currently studying these laws with a view to introducing them to Britain.

THE WEATHER

Apart from abolishing January and February, the British climate will be improved by towing the British Isles into the Atlantic and re-siting it 500 miles further south. This massive enterprise will have numerous fringe benefits:

* The revival of British ship-yards to build a sufficient number of tugs.
* A huge expansion of the British wine-growing industry. (This may upset the French but who cares?)
* The doubling of the size of the North Sea, which would re-juvenate the fishing industry.
* The disappearance of the English Channel, one of the most congested and dangerous stretches of water in the world.
* The re-building of the Channel Tunnel in rubber so that it could stretch further and link in with Guernsey and Jersey making the U.K. a tax haven and undercutting Switzerland.

PENSIONERS

* We will introduce retirement at 55.
* Pensions will be fixed at 100% of MPs' salaries (except for retired politicians, who've already bled the country dry).
* Military bases will be converted into Action Theme Parks where pensioners can re-live their war exploits.

QUESTION TIME

These are the questions that Loony candidates get asked most often

Q. Who funds the Official Monster Raving Loony Party

A. The Official Monster Raving Loony Party is self-funded by Lord Sutch's Rock 'n' Roll gigs. This means we pay for our own policies. Not so the other unofficial parties, who accept money from businessmen (some of them crooked, some of them foreign few of them not seeking something) or Trade Unions (sometimes as motivated as businessmen).

Q. How come you haven't persuaded enough people to vote Loony to win a single seat?

A. But we have. Lord Sutch alone has secured 16,000 votes. If only we could get all of them together in the same place on the same day, he'd win a seat in Parliament easily. As for Council seats we already have six councillors and one Deputy Lord Mayor (Ashburton, Devon).

Q. Why didn't you form an Alliance with the SDP?

A. Because we didn't trust a bunch of claret-swilling refugees from the Labour Party.
In fact one of the proudest Loony achievements was the destruction of the SDP. It was Lord Sutch's victory in the 1990 Bootle by-election - when he polled twice as many votes as the SDP candidate - that finally persuaded 'Doctor' David Owen to abandon British politics and retire to Yugoslavia.

TAXATION

* Income tax was introduced nearly two hundred years ago to pay for the Napoleonic Wars. These have now finished and at present we have no plans to go to war with France - therefore income tax will be abolished.
* Similarly VAT was increased by Norman Lamont to make the Poll Tax less unpopular. The Poll Tax is now finished so there's no excuse for VAT remaining at 17·5%.
* If we do have to have income tax, we propose to incorporate it into the National Lottery so at least you stand a chance of winning your money back.

OPEN GOVERNMENT

* Parliament will be set on wheels so it can drive around the country and be made more accessible to the people. It can even go to Scotland. For some reason the Scots keep going on about having their own Parliament. Under our proposals they can borrow ours.
* The home telephone numbers of all elected officials in national and local government will be made available to their electors so that you can have a chat with them whenever you want to.
* We'll also include in this list the home numbers of the heads of all the utilities, so you can have a chat about your bills directly with the people getting your money.

QUESTION TIME (CONT)

Q. **Will Lord Sutch - as a peer of the realm - be allowed to take his seat in the House of Commons?**

A. Once he's been elected Prime Minister, Lord Sutch can do what the hell he wants.

Q. **Is a Loony vote a wasted vote?**

A. Yes. But what else were you going to use it for?

Q. **Have you done your sums and worked out how much your policies will cost the country and how they will be financed?**

A. Yes. But it's too complicated to explain here. You're just going to have to trust us on this one.

Q. **What's in it for me? How will I benefit when the Loonies get elected.**

A. The bookmaker Mr William Hill is offering odds of ten million to one against Lord Sutch being the next prime minister - the highest odds he has ever offered on anything. If you're quick about it you could get a couple of quid on him now and retire the day after the election.
After all, you stand more chance than you do with the National Lottery. In addition Lord Sutch promises to honour all £1 million notes when he becomes Prime Minister - so cut out your £1 million pound note on page 14. Take it to No. 10 and Lord Sutch will show you round the place serve you tea and biscuits and cash it for you.

The Eleven Plus was abolished when it was discovered that not even the Deputy Leader of the Labour Party could spell 'willy'.

EDUCATION

We successfully campaigned for the abolition of the 11 plus. But standards in education are important.

* We will introduce lead free pencils.
* We will introduce selection and streaming in evening classes.
* We will make sure that there is a grammar book in every town.
* We believe in the Four Rs: reading, writing and rock & roll.

THE UNOFFICIAL LOONY PARTIES

THE LOONY LEFT

The Socialist Labour Party
Sole proprietor: Arthur Scargill. A one-man party dreaming of a one-party state.

The SWP
Space-ship worshippers who spend their time hanging around tube stations selling their newspaper 'The Spaced Outworker'.

Sinn Fein
Field fewer candidates in general elections than we do. Probably can't afford the deposits.

The Revolutionary Socialist Vampires Party (RSVP)
Motto: Better red than undead.

The Green Party
Used to be called The Ecology Party, but after the victory of Jeremy Stooks - our Official Monster Raving Green Chicken Alliance candidate - in the 1983 general election, they changed their name.

TRANSPORT

* Roads will be dug up a maximum of once every ten years. Before they're dug up, all the utilities will be informed and they can replace all their cables, pipes and sewers at the same time.

  Street parties will be held to celebrate the event and twinning ceremonies will be encouraged with roadworks in other parts of the country.

* All urban streets will have pram lanes.

* It's unfair that only zebras get crossings in the road - we shall give all animals their own crossings, starting with leopards.

* All dogs will be fed with fluorescent food so that nobody steps in messes in the dark.

* We're not entirely happy about policeman sleeping in the roads.

* All pavements will be heated in winter.

* Heavy plant crossing - has anyone ever seen one.

* Wheel-clamping is absurd.

UNEMPLOYMENT

The Tories have constantly changed the definition of unemployment to try to fool the rest of us that unemployment is going down. This is stupid! All you really have to do to halve the length of the dole queues is to adopt the Loony policy:

* Make everybody stand closer together.

THE RAVING RIGHT

'New' Labour
Stalinist dictatorship run by Tory Blur (the one with the receding hairline). Not as good as The New Seekers.

Liberal Democrats
Formerly the Liberal & Social Democrats (LSD). Traditionally they never had any definite policies and appealed to people who didn't really like politics - looking a bit vulnerable now that 'New' Labour is doing the same.

Alliance of Capitalists, Democrats & Christians (ACDC)
A loose coalition of deeply concerned and caring citizens who want capital punishment reintroduced for everyone who doesn't have a holiday cottage in the Algarve.

The Referendum Party
A serious organization and in no way a shallow piece of self-aggrandisement by a foreigner who's grown rich by breaking up companies and downsizing the workforce. It's not really cricket.

Scottish Nationalists
Don't like to be reminded that England beat Scotland 2-0 in the European Championship.

The Conservative Party
Deplorable lunatic fringe group who give politics a bad name.

MAD COWS

As the Official Monster Raving Loony Party we can speak with some authority on this issue. We've checked up on British cows and (apart from Ermintrude) they look sane enough to us.

We don't see why our animals should suffer just because the French are upset. We don't like their meat either, but we don't insist that all their horses should be shot. And we don't demand that all German vineyards should be torched just because they produce Liebfraumilch.

Still, as we're in Europe, we think we'd better make some sort of goodwill gesture to our neighbours. We therefore propose to withdraw all previous offers of mass slaughter, and instead select a single cow to be executed as a scape-goat.

We suggest holding a referendum in which the British people will be offered Choice A or Choice B, pictured opposite.

The people's choice would then be ritually slaughtered live on TV during the National Lottery.

The other candidate would be offered a seat in the House of Lords.

Choice A: Margaret

Choice B: Daisy

39

OUR LEADER - A BIOGRAPHY

 Once Lord Sutch is elected Prime Minister the tabloids will start printing all sorts of rubbish about him. So that you'll know what to believe and what to ignore, we are proud to present here a brief history of the man we call Our Leader.

Though he is now primarily known as a world statesman and as the consummate politician, Lord David Sutch first became famous as a rock & roll singer.

It is generally accepted that the field of popular music is even more corrupt and immoral than politics - anyone can have a hit record as long as their record company is prepared to throw enough money around. It is therefore to Lord Sutch's eternal credit that in nearly four decades of music, he has never had anything even remotely resembling a hit single. Despite releasing records as diverse as 'Jack the Ripper', 'Monster in Black Tights', 'Dracula's Daughter' and 'All Black and Hairy', he has never sold out to the forces of commercialism and sought the easy path of popularity.

This is all the more impressive when you look at the musicians who have queued up to work with him: people like Jimmy Page, Jeff Beck, Keith Moon, Nicky Hopkins, Freddie Starr, Ritchie Blackmore, John Bonham, Mitch Mitchell, Noel Redding and even Paul Nicholas all owe their careers to the early patronage of Lord Sutch.

In 1993 Lord Sutch was awarded a knighthood for his services to politics. Under the rules of compulsory competitive tendering, this ceremony was carried out by a private contractor, T. C. Owen (Bananaman).

From his first appearance at the legendary Two Is coffee bar in 1960, Sutch has been an innovator. He had long hair before The Beatles, made one of the first ever videos in 1962 and was blending horror and rock & roll before The Damned and The Cramps were even born.

In the 70s his influence as a patron of the avant-garde continued. He commissioned clothes from Vivien Westwood (including his first leopard-skin suit) before anyone else had ever heard of her, and gave the Sex Pistols their first ever gigs - they were supporting him, of course.

The 80s saw him courted by yet another generation of rock stars including Pat Travers and Cheap Trick's Rick Nielson. But by now politics was occupying more of his time than rock & roll.

The first opportunity of his new career came back in 1963 when Harold Macmillan was still Prime Minister. John Profumo - as though anyone needed reminding - had been caught sleeping with a prostitute, jeopardizing the security of the nation and lying to the House of Commons; he had therefore been forced to resign, since such behaviour was considered unacceptable for MPs in the 'swinging' 60s.

In the ensuing Stratford-upon-Avon by-election Sutch stood as the National Teenage Party candidate, campaigning for 'Votes at 18'. The minimum age at the time was 21, which somewhat limited his immediate electorate.

When 'Harold' Wilson was elected Prime Minister in 1964 and failed to implement this policy, Sutch had no alternative but to press the point. In the 1966 election he stood in Wilson's own constituency and won 585 votes. This time Wilson got the message and changed the law to allow 18-year olds to vote.

But the concession was too little, too late - Sutch now had a taste for politics, and he has been fighting for his beliefs ever since.

Lord Sutch celebrates his achievement at successfully negotiating votes for 18-year olds after spending hours with 'Harold' Wilson in a smoke-filled room. 'What about a light then Harold?'

He stepped up his challenge to political orthodoxy by campaigning for Votes at 16, and heralded the modern disgust for unofficial politicians with his 1974 incarnation as the Go To Blazes Party.

In the early 80s Lord Sutch consolidated his political achievements with the launch of the Official Monster Raving Loony Party, fighting his first by-election under the new banner in 1983 at Bermondsey. Since then he has campaigned the length and breadth of the nation, taking the message of Loonyism to millions of electors. He has been invited to No. 10 for discussions with the unofficial prime minister John Major, he has been to Buckingham Palace and he has still consistently refused the temptations of a successful career as a rock star.

Victims of the unbeatable electoral machine that is the Official Monster Raving Loony Party have included Margaret Thatcher, Tony Benn and - in the 1992 general election - all three party leaders at once: John Major, Neil Kinnock and Paddy Ashdown. All have nothing but praise for the man they regard as Britain's most important and influential politician.

The results that appear in the media of Loony-contested elections are often distorted by the inability of our supporters to get down to the polling station, but in the 90s even this has been changing as the significance of the Party has become clear to more and more people: in 1994 Lord Sutch won a staggering 1114 votes in the Rotherham by-election, scoring 4.1% of the vote and almost saving his deposit.

There is only one conclusion:

THE FUTURE IS LOONY

THE LORD SUTCH FACT FILE

Favourite colour	Blue
Favourite drink	Tea and lager
Favourite city	London
Favourite country	America
Favourite occupation	Feeding the birds
Favourite singer	Little Richard, Ray Charles
	Chuck Berry, Elvis
Favourite band	Creedence Clearwater Revival
Favourite guitarist	Jimmy Page
	Ritchie Blackmore
	Jeff Beck
Favourite film	Citizen Kane, Maltese Falcon
	Treasure Island
Favourite actor	James Cagney
	Humphrey Bogart
Favourite book	Animal Farm
Favourite time	1 p.m.
Favourite car	Cadillac Coupe De Ville
Favourite sport	Boxing
Favourite boxer	Rocky Marciano, Mike Tyson
Favourite animal	Jack Russell terrier, Parrot
Hobbies	Collecting junk and records

THE PARLIAMENTARY ROAD TO SUTCHISM

The steadfast refusal of the Establishment to accept the people's verdict at the polls has led the Official Monster Raving Loony Party to attempt other approaches to parliament.

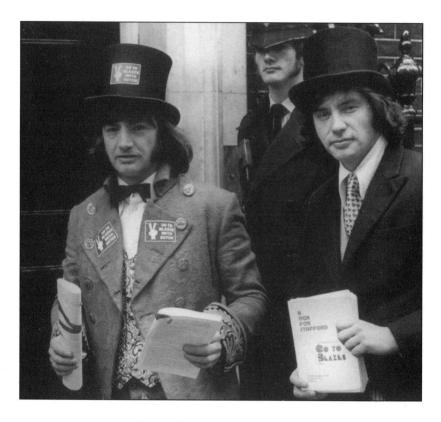

Stroll up and knock on door approach, 1963

Arrive in a Luton van approach, 1963

 Arrive on a Range Rover approach, 1992

The 12-ton armoured personnel carrier approach, 1995
-the Monster Munch

THE ROYAL FAMILY

The Official Monster Raving Loony Party is quite fond of the Royal Family, since they all seem to be loony as well. (and who else would make me Prime Minister). There is, however, some room for improvement:

* It's not right that only the Queen gets to do the ceremonial stuff like opening Parliament and sitting on a horse on her birthday. We think Princess Margaret should be given more of these duties, since she is clearly the embodiment of all that's best in Britain.
* It's unfair that only centenarians get messages from the Queen on their birthdays; we think that everyone should get a card on their birthday.
* State banquets at Buckingham Palace should stress the importance of British culture. Menus should be based on our national cuisine: spam, chopped luncheon meat, roly-poly pudding and Battenburg cake.
* We believe in Prince Edward.

INDUSTRIAL RELATIONS

* Strikes on trains and the underground will be banned. If the Unions wish to take industrial action, a National Holiday will be proclaimed for everyone except rail-workers - trains will run to a full timetable but will be empty, thus costing British Rail and London Underground millions in lost revenue whilst not hurting the public.

IS GOD A LOONY?

- If God were a Tory, we'd all look like Nicholas Soames and be born with an overdraft facility at Coutts.
- If God were 'New' Labour we'd all look like Simon Mayo, our children would all go to Eton and the National Lottery would be an Olympic sport.
- If God were 'Old' Labour, we'd all be made equal, able to run as fast as Linford Christie.
- If God were a Liberal Democrat, we'd all have Linford's lunchbox.

None of these are true, so therefore God must be a Loony.

Anyway if God isn't a Loony, how do you account for:

● Fat men who go to Test Matches dressed as chickens

● The penalty shoot-out

● Papa

● The no. 14 bus route

● Lady Olga Maitland

● Pantyhose

● Nicole

● Cliff Richard Christmas singles

● Amateur dramatics - 42nd Street performed in Bournemouth by dapple-bottomed housewives under the direction of a Scottish invert from Personnel Management

● Laboratoire Garnier

● Piers Morgan

● Jimmy Knapp's accent

A CIVIL SOCIETY

There is no doubt that behaviour in political and everyday life could be more polite in Britain. To raise standards we propose:

* All politicians should wear top hats - following the admirable example set by Lord Sutch - in an attempt to make them more civilized.
* National Road Rage Championships will be held every year on the Spaghetti Junction to enable motorists to express their anger in a controlled environment.
* When stuck in a lift nobody should breath more than four times a minute.

LOONY LAND

* When we win the general election, because Parliament will be travelling round the country, the site will be used for Loony Land, an exciting new development that will make Euro Disney look like a Mickey Mouse theme park.
* It will also have a luxury hotel where people can sleep officially

BROADCASTING

We called for commercial radio in the 60s. Now we advocate complete de-regulation of radio and TV. There will be only two rules:

* Anyone playing a Cliff Richard record will lose their licence. (especially his Greatest Wimbledon hits)
* It will be illegal to broadcast telephones and doorbells - it's so irritating when you get up to answer the phone and then realize it's only David Wickes in 'Eastenders' ringing one of his fancy women.

GOD'S LOONY SOUNDBITES

● **'God helps those who help themselves'** - This is not considered a legitimate defence when charged with shoplifting.

● **'Blessed are the meek'** - So how come Emo Phillips isn't as big a star as Jim Carrey, Chris Evans gets paid more than John Peel, and Frank Bruno gets his ass whupped by anyone with an American accent?

● **'Thou shalt not covet thy neighbour's ass'** - You haven't seen my neighbour's ass.

● **'Those whom God wishes to destroy, He first makes mad'** - Saddam Hussein hasn't been destroyed.

● **'A camel can't pass through the eye of a needle'** - It can if you get rid of all the space in the atoms.

● **'Man proposes, God disposes'** - or it might be 'God proposes, man disposes' - no one really knows because no one's quite sure what it means.

● **'Love thy neighbour'** - Well I don't know about love, but some people are quite fond of my neighbour's ass.

THE LOONINESS OF CREATION

● **The theory of evolution** - Billions of years of natural selection and what do we get? The Girlie Show.

● **The theory of relativity** - Best described by the popular rhyme:

There was a young lady called Bright
Who could travel faster than light.
She went out one day
In a relative way
And returned the previous night.

This is impossible as every six-year-old knows.

53

Mr Eddie 'The Eagle'
Edwards: the man who will be
Minister of Sport in the
first Loony government.
His first job will be to ski
down the European butter
mountains.

SPORT

* We propose the re-location of the European butter
  mountain to Britain so that our skiers have got some
  where to practise.
* We will build huge indoor jogging parks. People will be
  invited to jog on conveyor belts fitted up to electricity
  generators, thus providing cheap power for pensioners'
  homes.
* We believe a British man can win the Singles Title at
  Wimbledon - provided his opponent is blind-folded, and
  Cliff Richard doesn't show up.

- **Time's arrow goes the wrong way.** It would make more sense if we were born fully grown and then got smaller. Then all the Popes, Generals, Kings and politicians would be tiny, squeaking ten-inch tall midgets that we could carry around in our pockets.

- **The design of the human body is obviously faulty** - If our mouths were on top of our heads, we could put breakfast under our hats and eat it on the way to work.

- **Other loony parts of the body:** nostrils, adenoids, wisdom teeth, funny bones, knee caps, ginger body hair - in short, Chris Evans.

GOD'S LOONY SUPPORTERS

Lord Longford

King Canute

Whirling dervishes outside wailing walls (selling ice-cream)

Sue Barker

Little Lord Fauntleroy

General Franco

Cliff Richard

Welsh chapel fanatics

The von Trapp family

Guy Fawkes

Jehovah's Witnesses (even telesales operatives don't answer the door to Jehovah's Witnesses)

Ann Widdecombe

Orangemen

EUROPE

* We shall withdraw from the Eurovision Song Contest in protest at the unfair voting system that allows the Irish to win every year.
* We are deeply committed to holding a referendum on whether people want a referendum on Europe.

THE BIG IDEA (WE DON'T HAVE ONE)

Most politicians seem to know everything and have an opinion on every issue. We're different. We know that we don't know. We're quite prepared to accept that there are a great many questions that we don't have the answers to:

* Can't something be done about Barbara Cartland?
* Why is there only one Monopolies Commission?
* Why does toast always land butter side down?
* What was sliced bread the best invention since?
* Is Vinnie Jones really Welsh?
* Is there really a conspiracy by the security services to cover up UFO landings?
* Why is Cliff Richard?

If you can answer any of these problems, let us know and we'll invite you to write the next manifesto.

OTHER EVIDENCE FOR GOD'S LOONINESS

● **The lost tribes of Israel.** Who lost them? And how come God can't find them? (In fact the lost tribes turned up in Wales, where they live in stone huts under the ground, flay each other with leeks and think that Harry Secombe can sing.)

● **He gave the Devil all the best tunes,** keeping for himself only:

'Mistletoe and Wine'	'White Christmas'
'Kum Ba Ya'	'Tie a Yellow Ribbon'
'Brown Girl in the Ring'	'We are the World'

● **The Feeding of the Five Thousand** - Not even the British prison system under Michael Howard would try to feed five thousand people on fishpaste sandwiches.

FINAL PROOF OF GOD'S LOONIOSITY

In the face of all this evidence there can be only one conclusion:
God is indeed one Ghost short of a Trinity

DRINKING

We successfully campaigned for all-day pub opening. Now this has been adopted we propose:

*   All-night pub opening.

In an attempt to exclude us from parliament, no government has ever spent serious research money on developing a Morning After The Official Monster Raving Loony Victory Party Hangover Pill. Once in power we will have this pill freely available in all chemists. The benefits will be enormous:

*   Hangovers will be a thing of the past.
*   We will be guaranteed a victory at every election.
*   Millions of work-days currently lost through over-celebration at other events will be saved - Britain's productivity would increase by a level of at least 10%.
*   Industrial accidents will be massively reduced.
*   The NHS would be self-funded from the royalties generated by worldwide sales of the Loony Hangover Pill.

THE MINISTRY OF NOSTALGIA

We will remind people of how good things used to be. Since no-one can now remember a time when things were good, we all need help to dream of a wonderful by-gone age when everyone was paid in golden sovereigns, no-one was ill or died, the weather was perfect, and you could get 200 pints of bitter for a quid.

BALLOT-PAPER

For those of you who have never been sober enough to find a poll booth before, this is what a ballot-paper looks like.

Make sure you put a cross in the right box.

	VOTE FOR ONE CANDIDATE ONLY	
1	**ESTATE-AGENT** (Simon Estate-Agent, of Dunvotin, Sandal Close, Beardton, Liberal Democrats)	
2	**FFORBES** (Benjamin Quentin Augustus fforbes-ffrobisher-ffranklin, of 8 Granita Passage, Islington, London, 'New' Labour)	
3	**FRANCO-MUSSOLINI** (Adolf Franco-Mussolini, of The Bunker, Bergkampstrasse, Little Berlin-on-Sea, Keep Britain British)	
4	**GOLDSCHMIDT** (James Goldschmidt, of 4 Inca Drive, Mexico, Pudendum Party)	
5	**HOBBIT** (Diana Hobbit, of 27 Gaia Avenue, Peckham West, 'London', Green Party)	
6	**MARMOSET** (Sir Giles St John Marigold Marmoset, of Marmoset House, Pall Mall, London, Conservative Party)	
7	**SUTCH** (Screaming Lord Sutch, of Castle Sutch, New Transylvania, Surrey, Official Monster Raving Loony Party)	**X**
8	**SPARTACUS** (Rosa Spartacus, of no fixed abode, Space Workers Party)	
9	**YUSSUF** (Cat Stevens, of Ayatollah Drive, Tehran, Witch Bedouin Party)	

THE CITIZEN'S CHARTER

We're not entirely sure what this is at the moment, but it seems like it might be a good idea if it was extended a bit. Citizens should:

* Have the right to be citizens - at the moment we're subjects of the Queen.
* Be able to challenge politicians to prove that they have done what they said they were going to do in their election manifestos.
* Not be obliged to do anything at all before lunch, let alone go to work - it's too difficult.
* Have the right to vote for the Prime Minister (we wouldn't have chosen John Major, for a start).

SEX AND ROCK & ROLL

None of this has anything to do with politicians. Therefore all laws restricting people's private activities and their right to go to a rave (even if they listen to 'repetitive beats') should be repealed.

Under a Loony government sex and rock & roll will be available through the NHS.

THE BEEF MOUNTAIN

OK we admit it - even Loonies can't find anyone who wants it. So we propose The EuroSausage - one part beef, one part butter, one part wine, three parts hot air. This giant EuroSausage we would launch into space - the first EuroUfo!

Designed by Sutchy & Sutchy

TOO LOONY FOR US

We like to think that in the Official Monster Raving Loony Party, we are responsible and mainstream politicians. We are, if you like, One-Nation Loonies.

But there are other, more sinister Loonies around, many of whom have forced their extremist brand of Loonyism on the country with a series of pernicious laws and potential laws. We would ensure that these evil regulations are removed from the statute books.

This is the kind of thing that goes too far for us:

● Wheel-clamping is the most pointless exercise in traffic control yet devised.

● British libel laws are absurdly draconian.

● The Prevention of Terrorism Act does not prevent terrorism.

● It is illegal for London cab-drivers to brighten up their cabs with Christmas decorations.

● The Cones Hot-Line.

● Privatising the Queen's corgis

LORD SUTCH'S ELECTION RESULTS IN FULL:

1963	Stratford, Warwickshire	209
1966	Huyton	585
1970	City of London & Westminster	142
1974	Stafford & Stone	351
1983	Bermondsey	97
1983	Darlington	374
1983	Finchley	235
1983	Penrith	412
1983	Chesterfield	178
1985	Brecon & Radnor	202
1986	Fulham	134
1986	Newcastle under Lyme	277
1988	Kensington	61
1988	Glasgow Govan	174
1988	Epping Forest	208
1989	Richmond, Yorkshire	167
1989	Vale of Glamorgan	266
1989	Vauxhall	106
1989	London Central (Euro Elections)	841
1990	Mid Staffordshire	336
1990	Bootle	310
1991	Ribble Valley	278
1991	Neath	263
1991	Monmouth	314
1991	Liverpool Walton	546
1992	Huntingdon	728
1992	Islwyn	547
1992	Yeovil	338
1993	Newbury	432
1993	Christchurch	404
1994	Rotherham	1114
1994	Bradford South	727
1994	Eastleigh	783
1995	Islwyn	506
1995	Perth & Kinross	586
1995	Littleborough & Saddleworth	782
1996	Hemsworth	652
1996	Staffordshire South East	506

Fact: On average only 0.0001% of Loony supporters are clear-headed enough to remember where the polling station is.

ELECTION NIGHT DINNER PARTIES

Apart from getting drunk and waiting to see if Peter Snow is finally going to implode with excitement, election nights are dull affairs. But this time you'll be able celebrate the victory of Lord Sutch and the Loonies, so why not invite some friends round for dinner in anticipation of the good times around the corner. We suggest the following menus:

CONSERVATIVE PARTY

Leak Soup

* * *

Edwina Curried Eggs

* * *

Roast Beef (English) or Slippery Jellied Eels
Privatised Yorkshire Water Puddings
non-Brussels sprouts

* * *

Blueberry Fool
Cabinet Pudding

drinks: Blue Nun, San Miguel (for Michael Portaloo)

cocktail: Everton Blue
(gin, blue curacao, creme de banane, cream lemon juice)

'NEW' LABOUR

Gordon Brown Windsor Soup

* * *

Disillusioned Tory Bloaters

* * *

Boiled Bull & Carrots or Jugged hare
(in honour of the rapidly balding Tony Blair)
'New' potatoes
Red cabbage

* * *

Clare Shortbread
Garibaldi Blair Biscuits

drink: Beaujolais Nouveau

cocktail: Red Sunset
(mandarin brandy and milk)

As you're a supporter of the Official Monster Raving Loony Party, however, you probably won't be needing any of these. So try a Loony menu instead:

Marichino cherries
(on sticks)

* * *

Steak & Kidney Pie

* * *

Jelly & Ice cream
(with hundreds and thousands)

* * *

Bananas and custard

drinks: alcoholic lemonade, alcoholic ginger beer, tea

ELECTION NIGHT ENTERTAINMENTS

To keep yourself entertained whilst watching the results, here's a join-the-dots game for you to play.

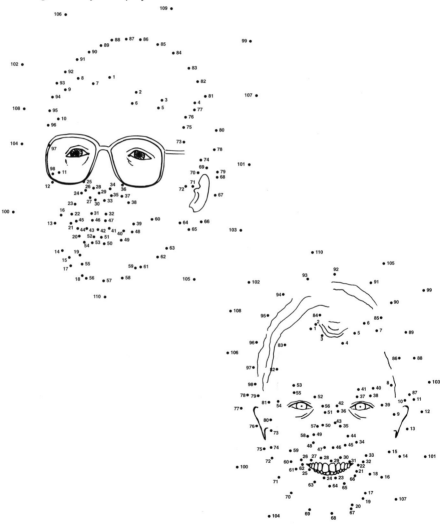

Extend the line by one dot for every three seats won by the relevant party leader. The first face to be completed has won 330 seats - an outright majority in the House of Commons - and is the new prime minister.
(If it's not Lord Sutch, demand a recount.)

FILMS FOR ELECTION NIGHT

The Care Blair Movie

A Returning Officer and a Gentleman

Love Tory

A Funny Thing Happened on the Way to the Quorum

Twister

Robin Cook - Prince of Thieves

North by North-Westminster

The Truth About Cats and Hoggs

The Prime Minister of Miss Jean Brodie

Michael Howard's End

The Big Sleep

DANCES FOR ELECTION NIGHT

The Quango

The Cabinet Re-Shuffle

The Pollka

The Mandelson

The Monster Mash

MUSIC FOR ELECTION NIGHT

Trains and Votes and Planes

Eighteen with a Ballot

I Only Have Franchise For You

Post Horn Gallup

I Wanna be Erected

I'd Rather Jack (Straw)

Gummertime Blues

Let the Good Times Poll

Can the Canvass

Mad Cows and Englishmen

Cockles and Brussels

I'm Still Standing

GAMES TO PLAY ON ELECTION NIGHT

Ex-chequers

Ballot-Boxing

Monopolilly

Trivial Pursuit

UNI-BABBLE

Formerly known as polybabble (until the exciting Tory reforms of higher education), this is a private language spoken only by politicians. You'll be getting a lot of this during the campaign, so here's a glossary of the key uni-babble terms:

All-party consensus

Situation where all senior politicians agree a subject should never be discussed in public for fear of upsetting wives and servants. Exists on subjects where the public overwhelmingly support an anti-establishment position: e.g. legalisation of soft drugs, abolition of the monarchy, restoration of capital punishment etc.

Back to Basics

Back to the drawing-board

Bastards

When used by John Major, this means Eurosceptic Tories; when used by anyone else, it just means Tories

Books, the

'New' Labour's excuse for not saying how much they'd increase tax: 'We haven't had a chance to look at the books yet'

Choice

Function of wealth

Citizens' Charter

John Major's big idea; main effect is that rail passengers and NHS patients are all now referred to as 'customers'

Constitutional reform

'New' Labour believes that having hereditary peers sitting in the House of Lords is an absurd anachronism, and they should be replaced by people appointed by Tony Blair; the hereditary monarchy, on the other hand, is perfectly reasonable

Corruption	see 'Hot potato'
Defence cuts	Reducing the number of musicians in military bands in order to buy bigger weapons; always ends up costing more money
Devolution	Proposal that the Scots shouldn't have as many MPs in Westminster as they do at the moment
Education	The only Liberal policy anyone knows is that they'd 'put a penny on income tax to fund education' - it works at about £3 a week for an average wage-earner
Electoral reform	The current electoral system gives the Liberal Democrats a disproportionately low representation in parliament; no-one cares much
Europe	The issue on which all parties are apparently 'split from top to bottom' - i.e. Michael Heseltine and Michael Portillo don't agree with each other
Europhiles	Tory MPs who think that Ted Heath talked a lot of sense, but should never have given up the band
Eurosceptics	Tory MPs who think that Enoch Powell talked a lot of sense
Falling unemployment	Astonishingly unemployment has now been falling for sixteen consecutive years (allowing for seasonal adjustments)
Fat cats	Formerly a term of abuse for over-paid businessmen; since the MPs awarded them selves a massive pay rise, the expression has seldom been heard

Feelgood factor	Currently lost; will probably turn up with the Holy Grail, the Philosopher's Stone and the Elixir of Life in a British Rail left luggage office
Freedom of the press	Worth a try - it just might work
Heart of Europe	Where John Major wants Britain to be
Heart of Mongolia	Where Britain wants John Major to be
Hot potato	Drop it
League tables	Innovatory means of measuring performance of pubic services; not yet applied to politicians
National Health Service	The pride of the known universe; still plenty of room to cut waste, however
'New' Labour	Tony Blair
Old Labour	Michael Foot
Opinion polls	Completely unreliable and yet paradoxically the only way to formulate policy
Parental choice	The right of 'New' Labour politicians to send their sons to Eton and their daughters to Roedean
Party funding	see 'Hot potato'
Peace process	Low-level civil war
Rising prosperity	Astonishingly prosperity has now been rising for sixteen consecutive years (allowing for seasonal adjustments)

Single currency

Proposal that it would be much simpler if everyone in Europe used the German currency instead of lots of different ones; to avoid suspicions that this will mean German domination of Europe, the Deutschmark will be renamed the Reichsmark

Sleaze

see 'Hot potato'

Squeegee merchants

People who clean car windscreens; for some reason Jack Straw seems to regard them as being more evil than concentration camp guards

Stakeholder economy

'New' Labour's big idea; off the menu since the beef scare

Tabloid press

Pretending to be sympathetic to 'New' Labour; only 'New' Labour are fooled

Tartan tax

There used to be a beard tax once, but taxing tartan's going a bit far; presumably part of thinking the unthinkable

Tax-cuts

Taking 45% of the electorate's income for four years, then taking only 44% in the six months before an election

Thinking the unthinkable

Abolishing the welfare state to provide tax cuts

Think-tanks

Despite the name, this is where people think the unthinkable - being a difficult job, it is extremely well-paid

Training

Formerly known as education

Unthinking the thinkable

Maybe we'd be better off without politicians

THE NAMES TO WATCH OUT FOR

As Robin Day once observed, why should anyone listen to a here-today, gone-tomorrow politician? No reason at all, but unfortunately it's today not tomorrow, and given the media bias you're more likely to be hearing from the unofficial politicians than from the Loonies.

So to keep you in touch with who they all are, this is the probable cast list for the election campaign:

Ashdown, Paddy   In 1992 his popularity jumped 13% when he admitted to an affair with his secretary five years earlier; could poll well if he's done anything since that's worth talking about

Blair, Tony   Once hirsute member of rock supergroup Ugly Rumours

Bottomley, Virginia   Formerly a very popular Health Secretary, then Heritage Minister (unlike David Mellor, however, she is not known as Minister for Fun)

Brown, Gordon   Upright Scottish member who was widely tipped for the top post; now Tony Blair's closest confidante

Cook, Robin   Always described as a fearsome intellect and a forensic debater; seldom seen on TV however

Gummer, John   Formerly known as John Selwyn-Gummer; hero of the first mad cow scare

Harman, Harriet   She may be a politician but first and foremost she's a mother and it's perfectly reasonable that she wouldn't want her children to go to a smelly local comprehensive

Heseltine, Michael   Deputy prime minister in nothing but name

Howard, Michael   Possibly the most distinguished Home Secretary since Henry Brooke

Kennedy, Charles   Disappointingly fat

Lilly, Peter   Right-winger who keeps his nose clean

Livingstone, Ken   Along with Tony Banks, the only genuinely popular Labour MP; not often allowed out in public

Major, John   As Chancellor of the Exchequer took Britain into the ERM and caused the recession of the early 90s; but we've forgiven and forgotten

Mandelson, Peter   Widely credited with masterminding the triumphant 1987 and 1992 elections for Neil Kinnock, now due to do the same for Tony Blair

Mawhinney, Brian   Like Dr Paisley, Dr Mawhinney is proud to be an Ulsterman

Patten, Chris   One of the few highlights of the 1992 election was when Chris lost his seat; sadly he won't be able to do the same this time since he's busy making sure no poor Hong Kong citizens try to escape the communist jack boot

Portillo, Michael   Normally pronounced Miguel Portiyo - 110% British; despite initial worries when he was given the Defence portfolio, he seems to have made quite a good fist of it

Prescott, John   Widely seen as upholding the banner of traditional Labour (the ones who lost four elections in a row); mixes metaphors and gin & tonic with equal aplomb

Redwood, John   Rose to the dizzying heights of Welsh Secretary before deserting the sinking ship

Short, Clare   Actually we don't talk about Clare Short anymore

Straw, Jack   The beggars' friend

Sutch, Lord   Prime Minister Designate

Widdecombe, Ann   A useful figure for scaring naughty children

THE FIRST LOONY CABINET

Once Lord Sutch has been elected Prime Minister, his first task will be to select his cabinet. As this is intended to be a government of National Unity, following years of in-fighting and adversorial politics, we shall ensure that there aren't too many politicians in it.

The following appointments have already been scribbled down on the back of a fag packet:

Screaming Lord Sutch Prime Minister and First Lord of the Admiralty

Ken Dodd Chancellor of the Exchequer

Lester Piggott Deputy Chancellor

Bob Geldof Minister for Overseas Development

Eddie 'The Eagle' Edwards Sports Minister

Mystic Meg Minister for Weather & Treasury Forecasting

Rolf Harris Minister for Pets

Dale Winton Minister for Pets who win Prizes

Princess Diana HRH Queen of Hearts

The Queen Mum Minister for Nostalgia

Patrick Moore Minister for Ufos and Trainspotting .

Oliver Reed Secretary of State for Health and Fitness

Bernard Manning Minister for Culture

Frank Bruno Secretary of State for Education

Mr Blobby	Minister without Portfolio
Peter Lilley	Minister without Portillo
Richard Branson	Minister for Virgins
Cliff Richard	Minister for Fun
Paul Condom	Minister for Safe Sex
Rod Stewart	Minister for Wild Sex
Tom Jones	Minister for Underpants
Elton John	Minister for Window Boxes
Lily Savage	Chief Whip
John Major	Minister for Rock 'n' Roll

Mr Richard Branson and friend? - Not!

IF YOU ARE STILL UNDECIDED ABOUT VOTING FOR THE OFFICIAL MONSTER RAVING LOONY PARTY, JUST ASK YOURSELF THE FOLLOWING QUESTION:

WHAT HAVE MARGARET THATCHER AND JOHN MAJOR ACHIEVED FOR YOU IN THE LAST SEVENTEEN YEARS?

THE ANSWER IS ON PAGE 80.

MEMBERSHIP APPLICATION FORM

I wish to join the Official Monster Raving Loony Party. When accepted,
I agree to:

1. Wear my Loony badge with pride.
2. Keep my membership card with me at all times.
3. Put my Certificate of Sanity on the office/kitchen/toilet wall.
4. Put my car sticker in a prominent place.
5. Cherish my photograph of Screaming Lord Sutch.
6. Read and inwardly digest the latest policy statements.
7. Spend my Loony Million pound notes at whichever pub/shop/bank will take
   them

Signed _____

Name _____

Address _____

_____

Post code _____ Tel: _____

**If you are enrolling a friend/relative etc please print their name and
address carefully (we want to make sure the Certificate of Sanity is
printed correctly).**

Please send this application form for membership with your cheque/postal
order for £10.00 made payable to the Monster Raving Loony Party, to:

Chairman　　　　　　　　　　　　**Tel:　01364 652205**
Loonyversal Headquarters　　　　**Fax: 01364 653293**
Golden Lion Hotel
East Street
Ashburton
Devon TQ13 7AX